# Sonnets
## *Walking*
### the
# Great
# Divide

Cecil Welles

authorHOUSE®

*AuthorHouse™ UK*
*1663 Liberty Drive*
*Bloomington, IN 47403 USA*
*www.authorhouse.co.uk*
*Phone: 0800.197.4150*

*Published by AuthorHouse 02/10/2017*

*ISBN: 978-1-5246-7801-2 (sc)*
*ISBN: 978-1-5246-7802-9 (hc)*
*ISBN: 978-1-5246-7809-8 (e)*

# Contents

To my wife, my children,
and the soldiers with whom I served.

# Namaste

Walking the great divide, a narrow trace

Where I am barely able to put one foot

Before the other, I abdicate my place

And allow a passerby to walk through

With a sincere greeting. "Shalom aleikhum,"

I say. "Wa-Alaikum-Salaam," she rejoins,

And all is well, peace rests there, momentum

Comes for two human beings to conjoin

In harmony. She walks to the horizon,

Turns, smiles, and disappears in a mist

Of evening shadows from a setting sun

And a wisp of fog. I go but wish

That such a moment could be held and fixed

And never by time or distance eclipsed.

# Sanctuary

Burrowed deep, a room stands by itself,

A cul-de-sac for Diogenes to dwell.

Fusty prints and opus fill each shelf:

Sweet are musty pages gone stale.

A Quaker gun stands outside the door,

Aimed to stall intruders at the gate;

Merely a sign to all that implores

To leave this inner sanctum to its fate.

As soundless songs let scholars inquire

Less life's daily demons that protrude,

A new yearning spreads like wildfire

That never should one have to leave this room.

For pages of yester wisdom need the time

And sanctorum to fill recesses of our minds.

# Chances

In an abyss on a loan island roams,

With his simple wares, the ashy storm petrel.

A deep, engraved crevasse is his home

To escape an earthly danger of the gull.

A cloak that's black, a plain brown on his crown,

His simple tastes a monk would turn away.

He spends nights in his chasm with a frown,

For the gull threatens all tranquility.

Blown off course, a red phalarope stops.

Her bright rust-red brings Ashy from his hole.

Passing by, both their wings have touched,

And Ashy smiles for once with all his soul.

Passion ruling, he asks her for a dance,

For *aphrodisia* he'll give his life to chance.

# Governance

Matthew, striking balance, makes an entry
Of credits for the simple costs to dine.
An actuary, a cost-effective sentry,
Matthew does not see the need for wine.
He invites only other skimping creatures
In the line of work that he enjoys.
Assigned to reap from others what is Caesar's,
They respect the meager banquet he employs.
A new man enters Matthew's banal chambers
And asks the host, "Where has gone the wine?
For am I not of those ruled by Caesar
Who has paid you from the coffers of our lives?
Tax our toils if you think you must,
But do not turn our harvest then to dust!"

# Awakening

The crux of what I say cannot be said,

So vague this day's cosmic encounter!

Your wisdom, grace, and charm turned my head:

Harmony dawned where once I floundered.

Predestined paths always found my way,

Not thinking twice where to turn or move.

A boorish tyke, a suppliant to fate,

I see now that life made me its tool.

No more! Honor beats the call to arms,

Not for war or glory but to say

I heard when you rose to sound alarm:

I took heed before my days turn gray.

Each of us in passing sets the stage

For others' rigid lives to ricochet.

# Knowledge

She trifled with him, this coquette called knowledge.

Still, Pedagogue smiled as he followed her cue.

A mind once robust, a fettle that flourished,

Now far decayed for being her dupe.

Called teacher, he taught the sky is red,

For that's what she told him alone in the parlor.

As she laid her chemise down on his bed,

He belched this syllabus with profound ardor.

Alas, genuine horror from this deception

Was his own for not seeking what stood true.

Knowledge as knowledge was granted reception

Though truth bellowed loud that the sky's really blue.

Flawed wits are Pedagogue's constant bane,

Bar their first folly is not erred again.

# Tomorrow

His Honor E.M. Black had a custom

Of closing his courthouse down at half past four,

Until young, rancorous Angela Saxon

At half past four and one was at his door.

A bra-burning wench from Petaluma,

Without love for jazz or fish-fry afternoons,

She pissed off Justice Black from Tuscaloosa

Just by her Birkenstocks with wool pantaloons.

Arguments erupted, then ended abruptly

When paramour aroma filtered through the air.

The judge and she did a bit of cuddling:

A nine-month venture that ended with an heir,

Future of America with opaline skin,

A new Eve of peace through kindred blend.

# John

Your final summons left us melancholy.

I know, dearest friend, you found a peace

That pilots know when wafted, ascending,

Drifting to where earth and heaven meet.

I see you now take wing to final glory,

With thrust, load, and airspeed balanced; thus,

No drag dare inhibit this closing journey,

When pilots follow the beam to Olympus.

Ride the skies, wingman! Valhalla awaits you!

Bring on the sonic booms as you soar.

Let the Mach speeds serve as your coverture.

Then taxi to Abe's bosom for evermore.

A requiem for pilots is the vow

To find their final peace above the clouds.

# Blessed

A Triton mid minnows, viscount of the streets

Who, in the lap of luxury hand to mouth,

Resides where El Dorado and Golconda meet

Fleshpots of Egypt and others down and out.

An opulent beggar with a long purse,

A member of plutocracy of church mice.

Disease and hunger remain his curse,

And shame flushes with his pelf of lice.

No flash in the pan, he sits, cup extended,

Smudged hands set for pecuniary transactions.

He'll thrive as Midas if all's as intended

To feather his nest with Muscatel rations.

So many like him! I've stopped counting

These oxymora in our land of bounty.

# Judgment

Sodom in the heart, as miscreant I,

In flagrante delicto, arrant in thought,

Depraved what was chaste, my Sabine.

I, soul of mud, iniquitous, arrant,

Sought a scamp's course, a path to debasement,

Forgetting that I perhaps had a soul.

And as I proceeded toward this abjection

Your spirit showed bright, an elegant glow

To which I cared not, seeking abeyance

Of virtue, a congruous decorum:

Your taintlessness, constancy, chaste nonsense

Made what was due in this monstrous forum

As miscreant I, depraved youth it seems,

Remain knave incarnate in all your dreams.

# Spouse

Her nimbus, a great shroud of fluorescence
Surrounds my moods with radiant light.
Her warmth that melts the frost's nip is
In most somber hours a welcome sight.
A touch that softens a heart when hardened,
A voice that rouses new vigor when languid,
A munificent thought when times are Spartan,
She finds victory where one seems vanquished.
Is there no price for such a companion?
No lion in the sheep pen as others suffer!
No mother, no father, no sibling champions
A life as this woman has offered.
If wedlock is prison, as some hail
Then, blissfully, I will stay in jail.

# Jaundice

This subtle hue of constant separation,

By all other manner, each is cloned, alike,

Where bonds of communal desperation

Set tribal tones of black, brown, yellow, white.

Blind and possessed by jaundiced ideals,

Each sees chromatic change to existence.

No matter who they are or what they feel,

The tint of what they are states acceptance.

God used peroxide for some folks' dye,

For others a rainbow that brightens each day.

But voices of others, who flushed dark or light,

Call what God paints not beauty but stain.

Too many of us just wink and turn our backs

On the evils that others colorcast.

# Rug-Rats

Fabian tactics in the living room:

Rug-rats in defilade ready to strike!

Waste-high penumbrae wait to seal your doom

And charge with pelts and dirks and stabs and spikes.

Two powder kegs, taut catapults, projectiles

Aim for the kneecaps and await further bearing.

There's no way out from their stealth and guile,

But, then, who wants to. You sham no knowledge

Of what follows, though chipmunk laughter gleams

From the shadows, but stay for the barrage

To hear the victory song they sing.

Rebuff not their aggressions and forays.

In them you'll hear love's praises and accolades.

# Melancholia

Raptures of joyless moments are mantras

Of exultation, anguish that assents

To subscriptions of melancholia:

Cheerful dolor to which grief's hope consents.

The crest of this abyss, where hill meets vale,

Where dome of this basin rises then falls,

Is nadir of an apex that tells a tale

Where death's envoy portends life to us all.

Hope's grief then infers and says nothing

Of the depth to which we rise tip-top.

Only flood tides carry not what is something

And weighs heavy inner light and what is not.

Spasms of the heart may never rest

When rumination rivets on our distress.

# Women

A psychic scar etches in our memories,

Rutting deep, defacing a moment's thought,

A constant ghost that haunts every sensory,

A spirit rapping whom by now should not.

We usually are coxswain to our life forms,

But she yaws off every course we chose.

Whether starboard or port, we weather her storm,

Sail by, on or to the wind, we lose.

Ancient ledgers imbalanced by our blunders,

A present life tainted by what is past,

Our youthful acts left us far asunder:

Unfinished business we never took to task.

Though we're Sisyphus, it's not a stone we bear;

Rather, she stays in our thoughts and prayers.

# Integrity

A portal with a view of dual vistas:

One you are steadfast as Cabrillo's rock,

While second, a view of terra firma,

Where your essence rests deep within my heart.

Your sense makes you my lasting advocate

To whose constant counsel I often seek.

I know my words obscured are mere substrate,

But life's journey says you know when I speak.

Judge me if you must for my transgressions.

Hail wrath, brimstone, and heavenly scorn.

Turn deaf the words I pray, if that's the lesson,

But know that through dismay I am reborn.

Goddess of the moon, words not heard but praise

The "you" I feel and what that means these days.

# Voices

Voices dancing side-by-side, residing

Duplicative in cadence. Harmony

Perfectly tuned to reach all, comprising

Dormant souls, awaken once drowsy

Thoughts, to what's tranquil, luscious, sweet, serene.

Buoyed by fastidious words jabbering

An impressionist's embryonic scene.

Blurred far, but close lyrics clear and soothing

As lovers' words dripping like molasses,

A child's cry muted by Mother's humming,

Riotous peoples stilled by reason's lexis,

Honor's fire stoked by generals' prompting.

Devine, melodious voices that ring true

Breed the course of what we think and do.

# Heroes

Abuse reigns cheap on who carries the sword.

Home fronts consume what has been won and fought,

While industries of words ravage and devour

The praise, virtue, and glory that are sought.

Lonely any hero who's hero not

At home. Callous hands hammer mighty blows,

Chiseling away stories of battles fought,

Virtue and pride now eclipsed, no more a glow

In hearts of heroes burdened. Heroes not

For tribute as one's people turn from praise,

But rather gone to pasture's heroes' lot,

Glory withered, battered, as virtue frays.

Parades for all they've done, a bygone age,

For home fronts profit little from heroes' ways.

# Episode

Roma boys assigned purloin for pleasure,

Their sisters sold as sirloin for a fee.

Mothers wept and likewise were bewildered

By father tyrants pimping progenies.

Albanian tyrants disbursed top price,

Their motorcade of wares a Ringling display,

For Serbian tyrants who bought what's young, ripe,

To please Western tyrants with rented forays

Into debauching with licentious delights.

Enslaved youths' innocence lost in tyrants' lair!

Tears from mothers weeping! A child's fright!

Tyrants heard not weeping, nor cared of child's fear.

Why should tyrants have felt for those enslaved

When the story of tyrants lived tyrants' ways?

# Beleaguered

Twin attributes, burdens by psychosis,

Imaginary beasts' double envelopment

Against our sanity, an osmosis

Of any semblance of final contentment.

The first's humanity lost to four horses,

An apocalyptic harness reining us as prey;

The second, greed and lust, decrepit moral forces,

Flank our sense of justice: both beasts' draw play.

Amidst so much dreary disenchantment

Can faith's point source slay beasts? Trick tribulation?

Or are beasts and faith both fictitious bents

And mythos drives all our lamentations?

Fictions of our minds are tomorrow's runes

When today's whimpers are never impugned.

# Ataraxia

A halcyon moment when soulmates affirm,

On this fertile ground for sentiment,

Their heartfelt bond for the other in terms

Of eternal, supportive accouplement.

Odin's disciple saw Eros ascending,

A hard heart was a time left tender;

Clouds cast away, and sun rays descending

Gave hint all warriors should surrender

To peace of mind to see all's in accord

And not the warrior's vainglory.

So, Inamorato, Inamorata, two words

Rendered cudgels and sabers elusory.

Celestial blessings to this place and time

Where love's armistice gave us refuge in kind.

# Kaput

Goblins in the pantry dub inanity.

Now, vexed groundhogs burrow deep snuggeries

And build pergolas against perfidy,

As well the coming morrow's skullduggery.

Chimera in pinstripes see utopia

In fruits of labor, coin purse, and hearthstone;

Fine feathers adorn these Wall Street brahmas,

And humbug for poor and plundered careworn.

Messiah politicos of groundhogs' making,

Sanguine spirits with rose-colored vows

Of celibacy when acting toward purse strings,

Ask all to have faith in what's said now.

Yet promises not of riches but repair

Work best to agitate against despair.

# Oh

Some with oh faces, then came Cheshire grins.

Some dour pusses, red with shame, gave naught

An inch to, oh, the young dawn coming in.

Oh, such aspirations this new thing brought!

Oh, how America's collective angels sought

To hold a communion and voice their will.

Oh, how justice speaks so clearly, I thought,

When it speaks with the voices from dale and vil,

Ghetto and high-rise, farmland and pasture,

Chateau and cottage, and Park Avenue.

Folks stepping from double-wides are enraptured

With the promise that justice will come true.

Oh, how one man called all angels to sing,

Not red with shame but to let freedom ring.

# Walking

Some proceed with balls first, toes forth, knees bent;

Others strut with certainty, shoulders squared.

Some study the ground, heels first, with intent:

Chicks on the move! Let all be prepared!

Shanks buttressing torsos like apples,

Columns support others like Georgia pines,

Moving in tandem, "dodu" and willow:

All shapes and sizes, yet chicks so refined.

Onrush of grace and alluring symmetries

Beckon gentlemen radars to lock in.

Panting canines beware, lest these banshees

Turn hearts to greenbriers of love, less from sin.

It's not the way the shapes and curves are built

But how their saunter writhes, turns, and tilts.

# Areolas

Fine lines define curves to what is divine

While each breath lifts divinity to new heights.

Twin parabolas, vertexes aligned

In minuet for two, dance a cadenced rite.

Cosmos's liturgy, two in communion,

Bring to light a sublime incarnation.

This flesh of the body, this bread of heaven,

Mesmerizes with nature's incantation.

So, truly humbled, in genuflection,

Where no soul proclaims psalms of rapture,

I sit in reverence for this confection:

Silent vigil is my sole enacture.

How I love the life these two adorn!

With each rise of a vertex, I'm reborn.

# Hubris

Achilles, drenched in once excessive pride,
Found comfort in another man's misfortune.
In Hector's desecration, we surmise
A scrimping against lost self-devotion.
Or does longing to fill pride's nook left bare
Foretell, instead, of Nemesis's triumph?
Does Narcissus's yearning for what's not there
Agitate this hollow victory's carnage?
If all were blessed with Psyche's beauty rare
And Metis's acumen for what is not,
Then less there is of others to impair
And less for profit from what others lost.
But though not so, not honor but one's shame
Rests in this vainglory and barren fame.

# Diorama

The sun meanders through shadow lattices
From narrow streets and sandstone rooftops.
Children use the corners to urban edifices
To hide-and-seek away their day's romp.
Peddlers, barbers, and cobblers sell their wares
To muffled moms behind hijab's awning.
Imams intone peace in calls to prayer
For whom achieving peace remains daunting.
Soldiers find their place in bullets' orbit:
This market will set today's bloodlet stage.
Children's blown bodies soil mothers' curtains
By rockets from the mosque where Imams pray.
After, Imams chant peace for all held dear
Through a lattice of words within each prayer.

# Siren

A transient moment of melodic

Chitchat on the veranda, so I refrain

From cached thoughts of axiomatic

Details, rather relish each word proclaimed

By your voice. All lyrics to love's cadence

Are whirls of luster and awe that embrace.

All wit is lost to sonant and parlance,

All enraptured by each fetching phrase.

Life's proviso states I remain docile

To Lady Mesmer: a tyranny retained!

Life without could ne'er be reconciled,

A joyless path from which sound minds abstain.

Quiescent moments are tuned by perfect pitch.

Songbird that becalms leaves this man bewitched.

# Snookums

An old man pats her kindly on the fanny.

She turns and grins, a sparkle in her eye.

An aging lion, he guards her, staying canny

To any outside hunters passing by.

The bull teases her, a friendly game of tag:

Oh, the fun of gaming with best friends!

This rooster crows, to all; he loves this nag

In lieu of any other barnyard hens.

Years have creased vintage joy and pleasure

Into wrinkles seared by lustful fire.

Those who find that years add to love's rapture

Know such thrill 'tween soul mates that transpires.

Indeed, geriatrics full of prurient zest,

Find the touch, the dalliance, a constant quest.

# Memorial

Rest with God and the bosom of your family,

For though this day you've left us, you'll remain

That constant comet, dubbed loving memories,

Spawned in your loved ones forever and a day.

We note, while you're perched on Gabriel's wingspan,

A homily of life robust in its consumption

And of battles bravely fought when confronted.

A medal to all who wellnigh have your gumption!

From God's vestibule, a mere step from her atrium,

You see your life continue in our memories:

Your love and your battles will be your requiem,

Venues of your spirit, and your destiny.

Vade in pace! I pray you find tranquility

When with God and the bosom of your family.

When I am distant, whether many miles

Or just inches, yes, a mere breath away,

My heart breaks with a snap, without reconcile

Or mending but shatters whimsically

Across far off fields, hither here or there

Until I sense you are calling me.

And then I hunt those pieces for repair

To return to you, my serenity,

My peace. Just to your name my heart submits,

Like ascetics' prayers constantly chanted.

Without that prayer, I remain a wretch,

A cheerless puke, grim and demented.

A heart's steward, you nurture my feelings.

A soul's guardian, you are my well-being.

# Facebook

What but by happenstance I find your face

Seeded among a mural of millions.

Lines from hope and dread, joy and sadness trace

A kaleidoscope of life's impressions.

Ocular to mandible contours etch

Paths from love, betrayal, to love again.

While glamour and fire, with a gingered gist,

Allude to a life incessant, sustained.

Relentless that look, from across the page:

Spitting in any direction will do.

If any young bull cock draws swords, I wage,

Is to draw on Boudicca, all to his rue.

For some age nurtures just the fainthearted,

But for you in the mural, grit is imparted.

# Classmates

When surrounded by dark acts and despair,

When distance puts me in dungeons deep, secluded,

A string of fiber stretched thin, a thread bare

Bond to once home, to old friends once included

In a different dimension, a youth's narrow orb

Now near forgotten. Light's shimmer at dusk

When shadows prevail, obscure and absorb

What is illumined, a small ray, I trust,

Brings reminiscence where recall's taciturn.

For those of the orb I remain a name,

A faceless portrait, small weight for concern,

A standpoint in which derision's refrained,

As life for some is but a shadow play

Where each bit of light brings ease to the day.

# Lamb

What better bequeathed from Arete, Amor,

And their passion! Love's match yields a lamb.

Only two gods in corporate ardor

Could contrive such precious, translucent gems.

While Arete cossets and nurtures babe,

Amor clears life's umbrage and blazes roads

Best used to avoid Persephone's fate,

And aim toward what good fortune bodes.

Grasping moments both gods know are lost,

As lambs mature, enfeoffed to time and age,

They plead for seconds more at any cost

To love the lamb and keep all peril away.

Extend time mothers give in care so thorough

To groom lambs' use of roads fathers burrow!

# Pathfinder

Explorers of the soul trek unmarked lanes

As thickets of discontent mar their view.

Lifetimes' ill will dims what could light their way

For fate could deem they never start anew.

Serene gardens fresh with nature's treasures

Align the way for some left untroubled,

While desert trails leave some closely tethered

To few drops of life. So, we are humbled

By one who makes his way from the desert

And in one short life sows his own garden,

Basking in what is reaped from his efforts:

What great victory before God calls him!

It's not the time it takes when all's achieved

But what it takes to find eternal peace.

# Crusade

A patch of blue in the clouds up high:

A trapdoor to heaven. Through the overcast

I climb the beanstalk remaining in stride

So I may peek long before death's passed.

Reaching the breach and expecting wonder,

I look about me and find only sky.

Above though is another cloud cover

With a patch of blue toward which I climb

Up the beanstalk with great trepidation,

For little I know what waits up high.

Also feelings of anticipation

Compel me to search, traverse, and climb

Through this second door, where I find just sky.

Above me, though, there's overcast. I climb.

# Gethsemane

Too far distance false treasures to embrace

Where honor obstructs reaching rainbow's end.

Rather than for senses to fully deprecate

Duty's code, a word, seldom spoken, wins.

Words tipping some tongues are comfort and greed,

Reciprocal acts of love some transact,

Goals and aspirations measured in speed,

All sought to fulfill their selves. Or perhaps

These are penumbras that merely deceive

Those who deny there is a finer stance.

For when honor is lived, one comes to see

Rainbows are but dust, empty pixels cast

Like shadows, where beauty's seen but not grasped.

Give me honor and its virtues, I ask.

# Stammtisch

Village courtiers gathering en masse,

Ten or fewer, these Scalopus Rex rule

A postage stamp. Never a one dares ask

Of things outside their manors, miniscule

To gigantesque goings on life's autobahns.

Grotesque librettos, their day's episodes,

Regaled by all around pitchers and steins,

When tactile hairs and delicate noses

Sense the arrival of a refugee

From a valley or two away, distant

Enough so one's sans welcome committee,

Until the foreigner in an instant

Buys rounds of liquid joviality,

A brew that confounds all antipathy.

# Diphthong

Two strings plucked to one harmonious sound,

A single chirp from two birds a cappella.

Lovers entangled. Legs, arms, and torsos bound

Web-like, fusing spirits. Anathema

Are those searching two syllables in love,

As others seek dropsical affections.

And be still to cynics splitting hairs of

A deceived heart. Please, no condescension

On losing from emotions expended;

Stop such bitter platitudes. Watch and learn

How eternal bonds, as life intended,

Outlive any rudeness others may churn.

All note, chance made a dice roll a doublet

That now contrives a pure and perfect couplet.

# Post-Deployment

Weak young saplings at sunrise, when waking

Tired as bears in hibernation, wish for

An eternal womb, more appetizing

Than mess, or clear skies or the U-S-O.

Withered away the mind's realization

Of all but what's gone, a boat lost at sea

Unable to return home. The loved ones

Welcome bodies but not thoughts. They drift free

Like air. No compass, no navigation,

Only soft, gentle whistling in one's ears

From winds bellowing sails. The direction

Of these uncharted waters, it appears,

Remote, withdrawn, with no destination.

And it goes on without hesitation.

# Pax

She came upon a stagnant pool and looked

At her reflection, and beholding a sight

That proclaimed what her own contrivance cooked,

She cried condemnations and then took flight

To her home, a private chamber, solo,

To study her beauty in a mirror.

The stagnant pool, its reflection bellowed,

It shook the ground, it cursed with such furor,

That the lipstick melted, the rouge turned pale,

The eye shadow ran, while perfume stank.

Lamenting past follies, a plan prevailed

To mend what she lost with contrition faked.

But as we well know, cosmetics confide

The skin-deep pretty that's ugly inside.

# Carthage

Today's minions play tomorrow's kings
As shouts from street-side revelry triumphs
And guns forgo crosshairs on kith and kin.
There's a moment's glory as patriarchs
Egress to exile, their Saint Helena,
To the misbegotten's exaltations,
Who bow, cap in hand, to the arena
Staged by a mob soon to be forgotten.
As intervals in time bring to the fore
A new liege who, without hesitation,
Will nurture his own well-nigh long before
Others, the mob, despite expectations
Unless the children of Carthage tell all
Each empty belly's a clarion call.

# Backwards

Elvis and Michael are worshipped, not praised,

Are unrepentant sacreds, not prophets,

Human bling with shrines to immortalize,

Not demonize, canonize, not forget.

Others' epitaphs have no shine, no flash,

Visited by none, forever jaded,

Though life's script was love, gone, those once close, passed,

Once praised, not worshipped, so memory's faded.

Battlements of bones bleached by sun contain

Ranks on tiny epaulets, not statues,

While the sins of freaks stay where all remain

Besot, taken with their lack of virtue.

Many memorialize clowns in stone

But not the ones who matter; they're just gone!

# Seraphim

Alone the woodsman eats, alone he feasts,

After servicing his village with deeds,

As felling trees for walls, branches for wreaths,

Bark for paper, cones for kindling.

Alone the woodsman sits, not seeing

His Gabriels or Gabriellas. So many!

Alone he ponders, thoughts are wondering,

Where, by chance, does pleasant talk, if any,

Reside. But he does not sense angelic

Overwatch at close quarters, these beings

Reaching, beseeching; a town of clerics

Thanking him, praising him, and then asking

Why, by chance, does he sit in solitude

When he has seraphim in multitude.

# Spiral

Body bags were there 'fore we dropped our bombs,

'Fore we landed, 'fore Third of the Seventh

Tipped the spear, 'fore First Marines flanked right. Sons

And daughters died when the monster evened

Scores, ate his own, filled body bags with flesh

Of his own soldiers he shot in the back,

Of families piled by age, intermeshed

Atop the other, conveniently stacked

For history's inventory. We came.

We found them. Like strip-mining for copper,

We dug a mother lode of human remains,

While new body bags filled, from new monsters

Eating their own, evening scores, nurtured

In knowing it's their turn, it's their future.

# Seminarian

The many sides of God came not in a dream

But through eyes, words, gestures of earthly writ:

Through life with all its charms, complexity,

And manners of mentoring me to wit,

I gratefully acknowledge, thankfully,

A world of teachers. I, the student, blessed

By others' wisdom born across all seas

North, south, east, west of Nazareth,

The centrifuge for what back home suggests

Consummates the spiritual prize all seek.

Better yet, there is not the end of quests

But the perfect start that blends creatively

With what came 'fore and after shepherds sang,

Herod's soldiers lost their way, wise men came.

# Ogre

My apologies. Beauty saw the beast within

A fiend with angst from raising his ugly

Head too high, ambivalence for once again

Being a gargoyle, hardly cuddly,

Or sweet, or polite but a naughty turd,

A bozo, a pigheaded, obtuse crud.

So chagrin! So anal! A whiney bird!

A diabolical, idiotic dud!

Extraordinary, tragic remorse

Felt by this contrite, sorry-ass excuse

Of all men. No sane person should endorse

Such behavior, such growls, such a short fuse.

Ma'am, there's a prayer from this forlorn putz:

That you will still love me though I am nuts.

# Father

When your life makes way through heaven's door, then

Please remember this: for me you're Jerome

From whom I found strength in the desert, when

My will and mind persevered alone.

When past the gate and looking back at me,

Please take note of this: for me you're Ambrose

For whom to learn and teach made me to see

The straight and narrow through a crooked course.

When in a place where you will find your peace,

Please consider this: from you I learned to lead,

Like Gregory, others to build with ease

An edifice where souls gather and greet

In harmony. Like Doctors of the Church

Your sanctity survives through a child's birth.

# Last

Those with a compass true in its bearing,

But with direction that no others see,

Tread paths thread bare by ideas daring

Principles, not mere notions to please,

Where costs without benefit but with risk,

Pursuing a course not for joy but for right.

While these keepsakes of justice persist,

Beggars think not but for pennies denied.

When cupboards stand empty, they empty dreams,

Untended gardens quell hunger for truth,

And feeding masses with purity seems

Capricious, an uncharted azimuth.

But all is lost when gone the last stoic

By whom we register our heroics.

# Despoilment

We'll pinch your ass as we sign your check,

A lesser sum than he who works the same,

And if by chance our business should cut back,

You'll at last be first ... for severance pay.

No! You may not stop the stork midflight.

And no, again, we won't assist babe's care.

As garnish in our lives shaped to excite,

You will adorn yourself as we declare

Sovereignty remains outside your reach,

And if debauched justice will fail you.

We'll maul you with ugly words to impeach

Your repute: we malign what we sculpt, too!

Milady, coitus comes in many forms

Most men tend to learn from the day we're born.

# Nidnod

Heads slink north-south, an approving gesture

Toward each disembogued polyphonic fugue

Of hate. Eagerly we never censure

These televised minotaurs so imbued

With venom, all think the cudgels harmless:

So distingué this choral of contempt!

So avant-garde these fusillades of callous,

Malicious bile disgorged to merely rent

All the space left in our numbskull brains

To where there remains little room for thoughts.

So, yes, we say, unrepentant, unrestrained,

Without thinking it might all be just jot,

And tee-vee news minotaurs are ninnies

As many broadcast babes are daft hinnies.

# Pulpits

I hear the pontiffs bray pneumatic roars

Bitter to ears like sewers are to smell.

These regnant, gringo podges mewl their lore,

Like fairy tales, to milk sops. It is hell

But for a button, red and true, in hand

That quiets the sugarcoating of fodder.

No tempest in teacups, nor honey and

Milk for babes, nor maudlin soft-sawder,

Just the gentle breeze whistling silence.

Then, core and peripheries of my life,

None to whom a button refrains, speak, hence

It appears, fodder as pontiffs contrive.

So, I store the switch, this button, away

For now I must confront what pontiffs bray.

# Due

The old girl is tired. She went the distance:

A steeple chase before her wounds could heal.

What price she paid. Gallant at the instance

This noble steed buckled from the pike weald

By a perverse ideal. Just the same, she

Pursued the aggressive vermin. Finished,

Or not, her breath is shallow, prone to wheeze,

And her gait lifts low. What's to accomplish

Is more than any of her breed should bear.

People need to lead the girl to pasture,

Let her pasterns dance free, her shoulders square,

Her hind quarters strengthen, and her mane capture

The reflection from each rising sun, then

A healed America she'll be: strong, whole, one.

# Lieutenant

This dullard, not yet a gerontologist,

Thinks he has entered the meridian of life

To where he assumes he is wisdom's chronologist

From ventures made when but a tyke.

Women think him seasoned to perfection,

A lie he propagates to all younger than self.

Guide, vizier, soothsayer, Sufi sublime,

Proffering life's lessons, a sage's wealth

Of knowledge acquired from better days.

Oh, how he preaches a seasoned line,

This lad, pup, tadpole of fourteen and eight.

He votes, buys beer, asks women to recline

And whisper between gasps of ecstasy

He's General! Warrior! Fantasy.

# Mother

Quiet, genteel tempest in petticoats,

Genuine parvenu, flower, and scrap,

In war, peace, home or not, near or remote,

Is consummate nurturer, fighter, and hank

Who secures a child's stay sail directing

Life's progression. Now terrestrial, stellar

Soon enough, her words at times plumb in

Line with where the child goes, how he weathers

Each storm or calm seas, success or failure.

The death rattle heard in what she has said

Portends of a spiritual adventure

From which her shadow's whispers will instead

Speak volumes from a vantage point near God,

And the child still hears what's preferred or not.

# Suffix

When my life becomes a reliquary
Where the dust mites procreate allegro,
My walls adorned, enshrined, a martyry
Of cobwebs on the trophies and mildew
On certificates of glories past, where plaques
Engraved with triumphs blighted by amnesia,
Medals and awards, whose faded facades
Proliferate, stockpiled memorabilia
Among which a pinhole albedo
Reflecting one timeless approbation,
I embrace this token, this memento
Of a genuine realization
That escapes from inefficacy's clench
Was from who is forgotten hence.

# Imperator

Satyr without technique, a sad condition,

Can no longer bring the flower to rapture.

Lothario sans a lustful tradition,

Which in prior times wins and captures

The heart and desires, every thought and whim,

Essence of all consummates cries of joy.

But for Satyr now it seems to be the end,

An every move defeat, desire destroyed.

If satyr is what's lost, and power now denied,

And time has left wounds deep and sanguine,

What is now lost can never be contrived,

And what is lost cannot be regained.

When hegemons resist all Satyr's lusts,

All nations on the square can then adjust.

# Lists

A string of micro specs, things to be done,

Irreverent worship of composites

For naught, but become of all number one

Tied to a sacred oath of requisites

While passing by rests beauty, intimate

Fulfillment, and of all, a word forfeit

From the lexicon of what's existent:

Passion. Arrested, a concept now atrophied,

Never mentioned, old hat, saved only for last

After all else is said, all else is complete.

After all, what's contrite is fully cast.

What is done seems worth more than what is sweet.

Once imbued in a kiss or art that brings light

Is now seen as carnal, entertainment, spite.

# Locutory

Bird at a window sees in but not out

And talks to the world through the eye of a worm.

The other birds parley thus, so no doubt

With bricks of genius all build to conform

An edifice of knowledge, of insights,

To wit, or of not wit, it's hard to say,

But sure these cartographers of what's right

Will provide us road maps showing the way,

Pixel by pixel, a binary path.

Perhaps they are right, these postmod Platos,

If their cyber catchments are able to snatch

Truth's applets that strung together will show

That worms' eyes, though the size of a pixel,

Together solves life's ill-defined riddles.

# Pee-See

A tiny inchworm takes some precious time

To read Ayn Rand, after which, quite inspired,

He pursues a solo trek and climbs

A cyclone fence, to the top, past barbed wire,

Over and down, to an eight-lane freeway

To cross perpendicular humanity's

Sense of direction. Halfway he waylays

To squat and piss a speck of liquid waste

So irrelevant among cigarette butts,

Bubble gum wrappers, half-eaten candy.

But quickly "they" come and lay on the cuffs,

Drag him to face the throng, take the branding,

Feel ostracized, and though minute in act,

Learn what condemnation declares as fact.

# Could

They traveled on the road to Damascus

By way of Kiev. A collective wisdom

Blessed their lives, a demos lit florescence

Marked their path, thousands exhaled free air, then

They marched. The quest for a choice went public.

A solitary moment of being

Heard, seen, felt by a world considered sick

From the fuehrer's democratic smoke screen.

The world watched: all those armchair referees

Smelled the putrefy of despotic lies,

Yet, never so inclined to stand up and seize

The one instant that fate offers: a prize

Of telling despots their days are numbered

And demos will flourish unencumbered.

# Feathers

Snowbirds with broken wings walk but not fly,

Steady, syrup drip tempo to their pace,

They proceed forward just the same. Ask why,

And they tell you it's all to win the race

To a distant end. Ask where, and they say

Out there with a nod of their chinless beaks.

Ask when, and they say always, without breaks,

No ebb, just flow of time and changing space.

Songbirds sing of springtime to snowbirds' toil

And take a wing to shoulder snowbirds' weight.

Together both can fly, and thus they foil

Gravity's demands on a goal so great

To somewhere seeking something sometime,

But the two birds as one make it sublime.

# Prayer

Prayers for peace come easy, as for the poor,

The aging, the victims of man against man,

Nature against man, not to mention from war.

But for a friend, an unknowing servant

Of God, who shapes life conditions for others

To excel, is too hard to utter,

Shout out, mumble, or sing. To bother

God with silence seems a trivial mutter

Of inaudible campaigning for miracles.

So, the heart pains, as I am neither doctor,

Nor Messiah, nor magician. Spiritual

Mantras of helpless angst cease when I offer

A cue: if God brings this miracle to fore,

Could not the work of God's servant be restored?

# Dackels

A morning walk, they meander to where

Their noses take me to watch the sunrise

When I say good morning to God. And there

My day begins. The Dackels pull aside,

Guiding me back to our modest abode

Where they question with a fixed gaze, a wag,

And a postured stance, decisive in tone,

If I should remain or go, work or play,

Be of good cheer or whimper all day through,

Treat colleagues as magnificent spirits

Or as poor capital for what we do,

Waste the day away, put the mind to test …

Then, the knowing Dackels ask at sunset

If it's "Good ev'ning, God!" or be repentant.

# Octahedron

A flotilla of six water lilies,

Each with a pair of lecherous male frogs

Eyeing their focus, a sultry filly:

A dozen directrices aimed at the log

Where sits the pageant beauty, a shapely

Toad of translucent goo, a sparkling tone,

A fluorescence in the moonlight, hailing

With a come hither tune in baritone.

Twelve projectiles miss their aim as she moves

At Mach speeds defying the bull's-eye for

Creating a vertice, angle of love,

Paradise in tadpole making galore.

Love exhorts the mind toward lack of reason

Where bulls' trajectories lack precision.

# Harmonometer

I was impossible to keep, yet you're able.

My demons, layered deep, yet beneath you dug,

Excavating the impenetrable.

So brazen that you were my Freud, my Jung,

My Madonna in denim rolled in one.

With Birkenstocks on feet of an angel,

Random subject tee-shirts that loosely hung

On broad shoulders, and gentle arms cradled

Me as you sensed my black and brooding ways.

This West Coast beauty greeted these shadows

With a broom and dustpan, sweeping away

The smallest mites that, if missed, might follow

And embed themselves in microscopic quays

As embers in the closet waiting to inflame.

# Hubble-Bubble

Others thought it blithering hookah sounds,

But your words were more manna from wisdom.

Jingoistic proclamations abound

Of calculus, rituals of care, solemn

Squares, others' forms to how you think and do.

Euclidean walls were built to crisp sums,

But you always knew better, others were fools:

The world could not measure, even fathom,

That they were now the extinct dinosaurs,

Lumbering Dreadnaughtus walking straight paths,

Roaring precision's platitudes, therefore

You were demented, trivial, outcast.

But three raptors attacking flank and rear

Represents the autistic mind in gear.

# Harquebus

Never mind solemnity pondering
Alone, quietly watching laughter en masse
Aim for the stars. Know that he's wondering
If his aim was right, the walls were built as
Surefooted and secure. Umbrella grasped
Tightly, he awaits for raindrops of joy
To tell him that he did all that was asked.
It is the wondrous sounds of girls and boys,
Women and men, parents and their children
Expressing love, indulging in tranquility,
Without concern. Celestial moments
As these bond lovers, friends, and families.
Solemn with harquebus, he worships this day,
Though smiles rest inside and joy hides away.

# Corvine

They would not destroy it. Ghostly anguish

Bleeding from the walls, a foul perspiring

Of pain. Frightful screams continue to languish,

Like echoes from flocks of gulls devouring

An ocean of helpless schools of life.

And so he built it with Poe-like chambers,

A satanic retreat, torture's midwife,

Where humanity leaves quickly than rather

Aid and abet in what most histories

Fail to tell: that after the builder's dead

Conquerors would not end the misery

But lie in toto in the midwife's bed.

Each generation of newly empowered

Find it standing while the conquered cowers.

# Maya

You taught the rhythm of a different

World to one who marched to Shelley, Byron, Keats.

Eyes are opened, ears are attuned, mind is bent

To a part of home with such a beat

That bellows the gladness, sadness, badness

Of where we live, how we live, why we live

With our neighbors, our kin, and, yes no less,

Our fellow country folk. After, you give

The silence of your rage between the lines

So apparent yet so demure, so blunt

Yet so soft in eloquence, so sublime

Yet so to earth on what we lack yet we want.

In sum, you say coexistence of all

Determines a people's rise, not their fall.

# Taz

Giants come in many forms. One I found

To be a terror with his intellect,

A pit bull, tenacious, seeking to wound

Who's misbegotten, triggered to hunt, dissect

Those who desire to place what forefathers

Found, an Eden, into a polluted

Sump, freedom into noxious enclosures

Of souls, where creativity's diluted.

A king among his peers, he bled and led

With vision and pushed those to be as he:

To love God, kin, country, neighbors, and friends

With gentle means but always resolved, be

Guarded, against those conspiring to cease

Our nirvana, our School of Athens, peace.

# Abjuration

Lions in sheep's pastures cluster together

And declare fellow wolves loathsome carnivores.

Meat-eaters masticating each other

Demonize the morsels that they now gorge.

And when all is said and done, they will pick

At the bones of the beloved ancestors,

Deprecate their spirits, derogate, which

Sacred to the sheep most of all, the words,

Wisdom, and insights of generations.

The sheep will eat only grass stained by blood

From those consumed and bow to the lions'

Injunctions to foreswear what could or should

Be the sheep's abducing from the lion's roar,

Which compels the demos to end the gore.

# Quilt

Two angels sew a patch of charity:

The gift carries forward mending a fence.

Such microcosms of humanity,

Sometimes minute as two Higgs bosons, hence

Fold into another, a lattice weaved

Of profound peace, of justice unbridled,

Of equity unchallenged. Glimmers leave

Spotlights on these bonds once left idle,

Now enflamed by a second resurrection

Where Jesus chose not to come alone.

With him are angels of our contrivance,

All the millions past and present who own

The completed quilt, cross-sections fated

To leave the powerful baffled, castrated.

# Mood

Shall one cry from refused approbation?

If the world's homilies refuse one's name,

May it be one should bow in prostration

Or be one to go on and forego shame?

Interjections in the imperative

Express the frustrations of those thought great.

True, they claim, consider the merit of

How wondrous the gifts to the world of late.

Why do not all ingratiate, inquire

Those alone on their own pedestal stand?

Where are those who admire, or those inspired

By shadows of what the bewailed command?

Not to, 'fore verbs or preposition at end,

Will make moods speak truths. They'll condescend.

# Patronymics

It is perhaps the vagina. Despised

For being what she is not, for being

Not what she is, for not being so wise

As to not be what she is not. Seeing

The pitiful pantomime of shadows

That men cast, she dances to different

Tunes, casting her penumbra that harrow

The trails of heroes of past virtues, dent

Steel armor that guards male myths and glory,

And upturns the patriarchal whispers

That embellish their sins, their whoring,

Their ample love for brothers, not sisters

Who scour politics, are goddess in bed.

Far better generals, can that be said?

# Calculus

Note the dominance of their proboscis.

An extraordinary derivative,

Ratio of lies over time, dismissed

Sincerity, to the repetitive

Conviction that, if seems from the heart, truth

Prevails. Consensus gentium hears wrong,

This geodetic vector aims at where fools

Promote the deception. Fibs are prolonged.

Truth suggests courage. Then why the muzzles

Long and heavy, wet and drippy, wheezing.

So, decongestion's ethics. Then puzzle

Why integrals of lies to diminishing

Capacity: bigger lie means wee unit.

Tis true for politicos and their pundits.

# Sainthood

She found her path on way to Letnica,

A calling that quickened the ground below

The feet of all, great or small. So, she had

Humbled many with humility, cajoled

Charity from the rich with poverty,

Compelled peace on warriors and statesmen,

Propelled from her pate her authority.

From heart and intellect, this small paten

And chalice of body and blood defined

A pastorate as a dedication

To the most destitute, those left behind

By others more concerned with trifling

Nonism. With sheer will and spade in hand,

She strove to remove our heads from the sand.

# Almanac

Before morning nautical twilight breaks,

Plowmen walk the ground where furrows zigzag

As troupes. Not ready for maypoles to stake

Their claims of village horizons, time begs

To stretch its wings a dawn to dusk duration

That nourishes seeds, when hatchlings feed, and

Where love breeds. Farmers plant the rapeseed, from

Which the stalks fertilize the wheat, then

Ready fields for corn. The village clock bows

To rattles of tractor motors each hour

Each day, each month until daylight narrows

And plowmen bring in a last autumn score.

Harvests in Bavaria bring to mind

That a rhythm of life is quite refined.

# Nowhere

A place where one shit inside, lived outdoors,
And the Book of Revelations was unbound,
In a bog of filth and slime stayed these poor
Wretches finding neither God nor the sounds
Of Imams to implore a deity's
Prophet to come once more. The Mahdi was
Destined for elsewhere, never more to these
Condemned to hell. If evil men took pause,
They would have found a way, if their blessed Koran,
Not treated as paper waste, was understood,
Read on how humanity could ascend
Where evil descends forever not unearthed.
When anarchy is the norm then, what creates
An order by which humanity finds its place?

# Andante

I cannot walk the Cotswold without ayre

And madrigal on the brain, nor along

The Seine without motets chanting prayers.

A Salzburg string quartet is a mere response

To my inclination for a whistle

And a hum and a fugue bringing my mind

To pause, my thoughts to clear, my angst to still

As I attend to what labor assigns.

Gagaku, sangita, Weimar chorale

All call allegro to slow its gait.

For when what is must today forestalls

To tomorrow, the sound of hymns will elate.

My heart is a metronome that paces

To the rhythms of songs from past ages.

# Andromache

The queue of olive drab marches in step,
Single file, past flip-flops and summer hats,
Jingles of smartphones and clicks from tablets,
Briefcases and casual business-wear,
Little packs on wheels that resemble dogs,
Cats, or mice with names that rhyme with icky,
Flashy shirts with labels from exotica,
Snappy uniforms of pilots, crews, be
From any airline, any nation. But
One woman stands alone, watching the queue,
Knowing that one is not there, a name cut
From rosters, a flag-draped coffin his due.
Ramp ceremonies start in distant lands
But end at home where Andromache stands.

# Gluttony

The kopeck nurtures mother and not

The ruble. The peasant tills her land and

Not the lord. The worker toils, while fraught

With sweat and tears, and not mother's statesman.

Mother's statesmen and lords hoard the rubles,

Whereas peasants and workers earn the kopecks.

The land and factories make what is suited

For statesmen and lords, not workers, peasants,

Or mother herself. She is neglected,

Stripped of her birthright, mutilated,

Overworked, burglarized, never protected

By those so entrusted. Thus is her fate.

Watch. Once rubles are spent, kopecks stolen,

Tsars' progenies will crave neighbors' fortunes.

# Coupled

Avarice and narcissism, not like

Frick and Frack, Bonnie and Clyde, Jack and Jill,

Ying and Yang, Ben and Jen, Mamie and Ike,

Simon and Garfunkel, Crosby and Stills,

Nash and Young, George and Gracie, Pat and Mike,

Bill and Hilary, David and Bathsheba,

Hughes and Plath, B and B, Tonya and Spike,

Sartre and Simone, Cesar and Lucretia,

Darcy and Beth, Frida and Diego,

Dick and Liz, Abelard and Heloise,

Vickie and Albert, Jiang Qing and Mao,

John and June, Otis Lord and Emily,

Still pin moorings with whom one wakes, sleeps,

Not to mention with whom one earns one's keep.

# Decoupled

You-us gringos and ethnocentrism, like
Archie and Meathead, Adolph and Winston,
Hussein and Yazd, Khrushchev and Ike,
Lincoln and Davis, Rommel and Patton,
Giap and Johnson, Jesus and Pilate,
Lenin and Tsars, Lazar and Murad,
Wellington and Napoleon, Gingrich
And Clinton, sounds like divas and nut-bread,
Batsmen and Jokers, Burr and Hamilton,
Chiang Kai-Shek and Mao, Clark and King,
Hector and Achilles, Bush and Bin Laden,
Pericles and Sparta, Boers and Britain,
Undo the handshakes from which peace prospers,
Justice intercedes, and hate is conquered.

# Celebration

While sunsets suggest an end time for me,

I see all sunrises for those I clothed

With what little treasures of how to see,

With what thoughts of some value disclosed,

And with what love from the heart I could give.

Now gone these strong spirits, nested on their own,

Their search for a place in the world to live

Continues with sure steps, heads high, eyes honed

Toward where their hearts direct and their minds will.

My curse is that I cannot join their journey,

To cheer them on, to ring victory bells,

To show pride, to waltz in triumph's revelry.

To have children, see what they are being,

Is to live again. Such fortunate blessings!

# Girl-Child

Mother seeks greatness through daughter being queen.

Father struts with pride as daughter wears her crown.

Curls, ribbons, and patent-leather shoes seem

No longer routine for mere post-toddlers. Now

High heels tense the legs, thighs, and buttocks

As this four-eight angel wheels pelvic thrusts

At other moms and dads who judge and clock

The speed of her squats, shake of her false busts,

Mascara's deception of dilation,

Face painted flush, and how the voice projects

A beat, a mournful syncopation

Of squeals, moans, sighs, whimpers, groans that suggests

Calling it contest is a ruse. Denied

By all what's portrayed, the queen's glorified.

# Antecedent

They are, we are, she is, he is, you are,

I am the spirit that gives life meaning,

The clouds artistic beauty, water pleasure.

A looking-glass world in turn gives us feelings

Of how we call ourselves with a first name,

A last name, an "is am", a "sex-you-all-

Ee-tay", a job title, a heralded fame,

A fortune claimed that stutter, spit, and befall

An unpronounceable sound as many labels

Overlap, integrate, disintegrate

Into what is first now last, last enabled

To be first, and layered metamorphic slates

Where the essence of being is fuzzy, blurred

By labels, once flash, now like water, demure.

# Gravamen

To what magistrate do we state our case

When we lose respect of our endowment

To fix ourselves, grow lazy, and placate

Toward those who pledge us a free allowance?

To what jurist when fan fiction's truth, we numb

Our souls, our righteous sense, with its presence,

And to hate, fear, prejudice we succumb,

With which we pave over human progress?

To what tribunal when all those promises

That should only come from whom we fail to

Ask? Ourselves. Look in the mirror. Ominous

Proposition I know, see not to hail to:

Not the salesman with miracle cures,

Not the canticles that play on our fears.

# Lost

Another door closes. Death encircles.

Memories are jostled. Heartstrings are pulled.

Regrets are mobilized. Thank you stays furled.

A corner gathers dust where sits a lull,

From the day's action, a contemplation

Of friendship not regained, of lost moments

From a past, so efficient, dissipation

Of sour exclamations. Now, one laments.

Days turned to months, and months turned to decades

Of wanting to thaw the thick, layered ice,

That is, warm the shared pools in which we wade

Hand-in-hand. A mere smile would have sufficed

With the words, "no worries." But not this case,

The parting incurred retained its frozen face.

# Centerpiece

Ghosts visiting Pristina—Byzantium,

King Stefan, and Skenderbeg—sat for dinner,

Their feet resting atop an ottoman,

Their course a fig leaf, a dove, and ginger,

The last to calm the stomach's nausea

From tales of yesteryears' deprivations.

No longer should we weep for Illyria,

For the ghosts have lobbied for concatenation

Of all the hairs split ... and the children heard.

Each child's preferred confectionaries,

What's future not past, makes it understood

That what was once sufficient, ordinary

Explications no longer drives choices.

The narratives must match only young voices.

# Mouths

There are big ones, small ones, medium ones,

Some small ones with big teeth and sharp bite,

Some big ones with small teeth and no bite, some

Medium ones with flat teeth to gnaw just right.

Requiring asset management, it is

Never so. Demanding constant care,

Sometimes but not enough. Ivories

Whitened as pearl-like drops, an exterior

To hide its black depth of spiteful conveyance.

There are specialists to mend what's broken

And mitigate decay but no forbearance

To patch the wounds from what was spoken.

But to repair for all when we're remiss,

We seal a heart's uplifting with a kiss.

# Sengen-Sama

I continue, the great divide before me.

Each footstep I take inscribes monikers

To places and people and deities

Seen or felt or smelled or tasted or heard.

My path leads to a mountain, Fujiyama,

Atop where I'm greeted by a Kannushi,

But it's her I sense, her voice, touch, aroma

Consigning what I had not yet seen

That great victories, not mine, are for others,

Any glories will be in history

But not with my name. But I needn't wonder,

The monikers I lay, no mystery

To those who read, ensures my path provides

Others with a map of one story, one life.

9 781524 678029